Holka Polka

By

D. M. Larson

CAST OF CHARACTERS

(6+ female, 2+ male, 11+ either and optional extras)

BRENDA: A young good witch who is given the quest to save fairytale land.

WOLF: A misunderstood wolf who helps out BRENDA on her quest.

CINDY: A princess who has been tricked into thinking she is ugly.

HUMPTY: Humphrey Dumpty who pretends to be a mild mannered servant who is in reality a someone in disguise.

SPLENDA: The good witch of the South and BRENDA's mother.

EZI: CINDY's evil sister.

DEZI: CINDY's other evil sister.

FGM: The Fairy Godmother who has an evil plan.

PINOCCHIO: A servant of the PRINCE who is wooden boy with a nose that hurts.

PRINCE: He is a handsome guy who has been put under a sleep spell by someone.

SNORZ: An Italian wizard with the power to make someone sleep and is really the Fairy Godfather in disguise.

HILDA: The head witch who wants to save the magic in fairytale land.

GANDOLT: A wise wizard who wants to help save magic.

ZORKA: A wise-cracking witch.

SWEET: A witch who is the sister of the witch who had a run in with Hansel and Gretel.

INKANTADORA: A witch who sees the bad side to everything.

ZOOM: A witch who can't stop talking and gets turned into a toad.

GNOMES and GUARDS (these can be played by two or more actors and can be the same or different actors for each)

Additional WITCHES may also be added to the opening scene. If more speaking roles are desired the parts of ZORKA and INKANTADORA can't be split up into more WITCHES.

* * * * * * * * * * *

TIME AND PLACE
Once upon a time in fairytale land.

* * * * * * * * * * *

SCENE 1

(Witches gathered at meeting. Witches and wizards in
background can resemble famous ones from movies, books and
TV. Witches are all talking and cackling loudly)

                HILDA
        Hey, you witches. Quiet down.
            (All WITCHES continue to talk)
        Everyone quiet before I turn
        you all into toads!

(Talking dies down except for one witch ZOOM who keeps
talking about her new broom. HILDA goes over to her and
gives her the evil eye)

                ZOOM
        And this new broom I got has the
        coolest features. It can go 0 to 60
        in a scream and... (She stops and
        turns to see HILDA) Sorry! (HILDA
        pulls out her wand and ZOOM runs)
        No!

(ZOOM is off stage and HILDA waves her wand and there is a
boom and the lights go up and down. After a moment:)

                ZOOM (OFF)
        Ribbit!

                HILDA
        All right, you witches. We've got
        ourselves a serious PR problem
        here.

                ZORKA
        What do you mean?

                HILDA
        Witches have got a seriously bad
        reputation here in Fairy Tale land
        and it's only getting worse since
        the Hansel and Gretel incident. I
        mean, come on people. Eating
        children. That's just low.

(CONTINUED)

                         SWEET
          But they were eating my sister's
          house, Eating it! Can you believe
          it? I've heard of eating someone
          out of house and home but that's
          ridiculous.

                         HILDA
          That's what she gets for making her
          house out of candy.

                         SWEET
          But candy is the construction
          material of tomorrow. I'd bet my
          wand on it.

                         GRANDOLT
          So you witches have a problem then.
          Why do we wizards need to be here?

                         HILDA
          Because they're thinking of getting
          rid of all magic.

                         INKANTADORA
          What? They can't do that.

                         HILDA
          They can and they will unless we
          turn things around and prove we can
          handle having magic.

                         GRANDOLT
          Wait a minute. Who is saying they
          will take our magic?

                         HILDA
          The fairies.

(All witches and wizards respond in knowing disgust)

                         ZORKA
          The fairies. It figures.

                         INKANTADORA
          Can they really take our magic?

                         HILDA
          They gave it to fairytale land in
          the first place. And now they want
          it all back because they think we
          can't handle it.

                                              (CONTINUED)

                    SWEET
          That's so like them. All kind and
          giving and they make everyone all
          happy and then they snatch is away.

                    GRANDOLT
          So what do we do to keep our magic?

                    ZORKA
          Dress like fairies?

(ZORKA flitters around and witches cackle)

                    HILDA
          This is no time for jokes. We have
          a crisis here. I mean, what's a
          witch without her magic?

                    SWEET
          A really bad cook?

                    HILDA
          We're nothing, I tell you. We'll be
          just a bunch of old ladies!
          (GANDOLT clears his throat) And men
          with bad hair and skin.

                    SWEET
          I always thought I was pretty
          enough to be a fairy.

                    ZORKA
          Somebody's magic mirror has been
          lying to them.

(SWEET gives ZORKA a dirty look)

                    GANDOLT
          So what do we do, Hilda? How do we
          save our magic?

                    HILDA
          We have to do a major PR thing.
          Good deeds and stuff.

                    ZORKA
          Good deeds.

                    INKANTADORA
          We can't do that. It's so... not
          us.

                    HILDA
          Then say "poof" to your magic and
          learn to use chopsticks because
          that's all our wands will be good
          for.

                    GANDOLT
          Fine, fine. Tell us what we need to
          do, Hilda.

                    HILDA
          We need to do a good deed. Not just
          any good deed, but a whopper of a
          good one.

                    ZORKA
          I could let that one girl out of
          that tower?

                    SWEET
          And I could let those kids out of
          my cookie jar?

                    HILDA
          No, bigger. We're going to save the
          Prince.

                    ZORKA
          THE Prince?

                    INKANTADORA
          Oh, dear. The fairies won't like
          that.

                    HILDA
          But think of the PR. Witches saving
          the Prince. And before some bubble
          headed princess manages to do it.

                    GANDOLT
          So what's wrong with the Prince?

                    HILDA
          He's been put under a sleeping
          spell.

(ZORKA pokes SNORZ who wakes up. SNORZ is an old Italian
godfather type wizard)

                    SNORZ
          What? I didn't do it.

                              HILDA
          No, none of it did it. It may have
          been a fairy.

                              ZORKA
          A fairy turned bad, on the next
          Jerry Springer.

                              SNORZ
          So you want me to wake him up?

                              HILDA
          No, we need to do a whole makeover.
          We need to send the nicest, cutest
          witch we can find.

                              SWEET
          Well, if you insist.

                              INKANTADORA
          Oh, please.

                              ZORKA
          She's cute in the dark.

                              SWEET
          Why thank... hey!

                              GANDOLT
          So whom do you have in mind?

                              HILDA
          Well, I developed this little
          device...

(HILDA pulls out a long stick with a large meter on it that
has from "sweet" to "sour" printed on it)

                              ZORKA
          Sweet to Sour?

                              HILDA
          As you can see, I'm on the sour
          side. (Takes it over to SWEET) But
          when you hold it up to someone like
          this.

                              INKANTADORA
          Still sour.

                              SWEET
          No, that can't be. It must be
          broken.

                              HILDA
                    Well, it usually works.

                              GANDOLT
                    So have you tried this out?

                              HILDA
                    I have.

                              ZORKA
                    And?

                              HILDA
                    The sweetest witch is...

                              INKANTADORA
                    Oh, no. She's doing a dramatic
                    pause. This can't be good.

                              GANDOLT
                    Out with it, Hilda.

                              HILDA
                    Well, I went to the Good Witch of
                    the South's house...

                              INKANTADORA
                    Not Splenda.

                              ZORKA
                    I should have known she'd be the
                    sweetest.

                              HILDA
                    Actually no.

                              GANDOLT
                    Who can possibly be sweeter than
                    her?

                              HILDA
                    Her daughter, Brenda.

                              ZORKA
                    Brenda. What kind of name is that?
                    Not very witchy.

                              SWEET
                    It's so... common.

                              HILDA
                    I know, I know. But she registered
                    99.9% on the sweet meter. I've
                    asked her mother to bring her here.

                              ZORKA
                    I thought we were done with the
                    "good" witches. How can you be a
                    good witch anyway?

                              SWEET
                    I'm a good witch.

                              ZORKA
                    Until you get hungry.

                              SWEET
                    I don't cook children... much.

                              HILDA
                    So if there are no objections! (All
                    witches and wizards complain loudly
                    "I object") Well, then if there
                    aren't too many objections?

                              GANDOLT
                    Go ahead and bring her in.

                              HILDA
                    Splenda? We're ready for you now.

(There is sparkling light and happy music as SPLENDA enters.
SPLENDA smiles happily and speaks with almost a coo)

                              SPLENDA
                    Hello, everyone. It's lovely to see
                    you all.

(ZORKA makes a gagging motion like SPLENDA makes her ill)

                              HILDA
                    So Splenda. Will you give us your
                    first-born child?

                              SPLENDA
                    What?

(HILDA pulls out a book)

                              HILDA
                    Ooops. Sorry, wrong story. (Pulls
                    out a different book) Oh, yes, here
                    it is. Is your daughter Brenda
                    willing to go on a quest for us?

                              SPLENDA
                    She has consented to help.

                         HILDA
          Excellent. So send her in?

                         SPLENDA
          Not yet. I wish set a few rules
          first.

                         ZORKA
          Now she's sounding like a witch.

                         SPLENDA
          You must promise to keep Brenda
          safe from harm.

                         HILDA
          Done.

                         SPLENDA
          Splendid.

                         HILDA
          That all?

                         SPLENDA
          And not force her to do anything
          bad.

                         HILDA
          Fine.

                         SPLENDA
          Splendid.

                         HILDA
          Anything else?

                         SPLENDA
          And if she drops below 99.8 on the
          sweet and sour meter, she's coming
          home.

                         HILDA
          How about 99.1?

                         SPLENDA 99.7

                         HILDA
          99.5 and that's my final offer.

                         SPLENDA
          Splendid.

(CONTINUED)

                         ZORKA
          So this means we can make her .4%
          bad?

                         HILDA
          Quiet you.

                         SPLENDA
          Brenda. You may appear now.

(BRENDA walks in)

                         GANDOLT
          That wasn't very dramatic. Have her
          go back and try again.

                         SPLENDA
          She come in the most splendid way
          possible. Without drawing attention
          to herself.

                         ZORKA
          What fun is that?

                         HILDA
          So does she have any powers?

                         SPLENDA
          She might.

                         HILDA
          Might?

                         BRENDA
          I don't get to practice much.

                         HILDA
          You mean you haven't trained her?
          You haven't sent her to school?

                         SPLENDA
          In this day and age of magic being
          at an end, I don't see the point.

                         GANDOLT
          A witch without powers? This won't
          do at all.

                         BRENDA
          I have powers. I just don't like to
          show off.

                          HILDA
          I'd feel better if we had a little
          demo.

                          BRENDA
          Well, I'm not used to doing magic
          in front of so many people.

                          ZORKA
          Shall we all leave the room?

                          SWEET
          Close our eyes?

(Witches and wizards cackle)

                          SPLENDA
          Never mind, Brenda. Let's go. This
          was a bad idea.

                          HILDA
          No, wait. We'll take her as is. We
          just need someone nice. Not
          magical.

                          GANDOLT
          Not magical? Then how can she save
          the Prince?

(BRENDA is concerned)

                          BRENDA
          What happened to the Prince?

                          SNORZ
          Sleeping spell. And no, I didn't do
          it.

                          GANDOLT
          And how can she break the spell
          without magic?

                          BRENDA
          I have a little magic.

                          SNORZ
          Not powerful enough to break a
          sleeping spell!

                          SPLENDA
          You don't need magic. You just need
          a keen mind to ferret out the
          culprit.

                              ZORKA
          Huh?

                              BRENDA
          You mean like a detective? I'm a
          good detective.

                              SPLENDA
          Once you find the person who cast
          the spell, then you get her to
          break it.

                              INKANTADORA
          And how do you do that?

                              BRENDA
          Well, if we know who cast the
          spell, they'll be in danger of
          being turned in. But if you can get
          them to break the spell without
          anyone finding out... then she
          won't get in trouble and everything
          will be okay.

                              SPLENDA
          Splendid. Very smart.

                              HILDA
          And a little sneaky. She'll do.

                              SPLENDA
          That's the .1%. She gets it from
          her father.

                              SWEET
          That's what she thinks.

                              SPLENDA
          What was that, dear?

                              SWEET
          Oh, you're so artificial.

                              HILDA
          So Brenda? Are you ready?

                              BRENDA
          Let me get this straight. I either
          need to find out who put the Prince
          to sleep or find my own way of
          waking up the Prince.

                    GANDOLT
          Both is even better.

(GANDOLT pats her on the head and exits)

                    ZORKA
          Good luck, kid. Make us proud.

(ZORKA pats her hard on the back and exits)

                    SWEET
          She doesn't look so sweet to me.

(SWEET gives BRENDA a dirty look and exits)

                    INKANTADORA
          Don't get thrown in a hot spoiling
          pot... (Starts to go but stops) Or
          chopped up by some woodsman...
          (Starts to go but stops) Or get
          water thrown on you...

(HILDA chases INKANTADORA)

                    HILDA
          Just go, will you? All of you.

(Other witches and wizards exit except for HILDA, SPLENDA
and BRENDA)

                    SPLENDA
          Have a splendid time, dear.

                    BRENDA
          Okay.

                    SPLENDA
          And if you need anything, just tap
          your magenta mukluks together like
          so.

(SPLENDA demonstrates)

                    HILDA
          Magenta mukluks?

                    BRENDA
          Thanks, mother. Bye.

(SPLENDA glides out)

                                        (CONTINUED)

                        HILDA
            Thanks again, kid. Stay sweet.

                        BRENDA
            I'll try.

                        HILDA
            (Sighs and mumbles to herself as
            she leaves) "Stay sweet." Can't
            believe I just said that.

(HILDA exits)

                        BRENDA
            Wait, which way do I go? (But she's
            alone. She sighs and sits) Now
            what?

(SNORZ sneaks in looking nervous)

                        SNORZ
            Hey, kid. I've got something for
            you.

                        BRENDA
            What?

                        SNORZ
            I've got a potion that will break
            any sleeping spell.

                        BRENDA
            Great.

(SNORZ holds it out. BRENDA reaches but then he snatches it
away)

                        SNORZ
            Prepared to make a deal?

                        BRENDA
            Can't witches do anything without
            getting anything out of it?

                        SNORZ
            No.

                        BRENDA
            Didn't think so.

                        SNORZ
            You've got to promise me you'll get
            a piece of the Prince's hair.

                                              (CONTINUED)

                    BRENDA
          His hair?

                    SNORZ
          Or no potion.

                    BRENDA
          Well, that seems harmless enough.

                    SNORZ
          Promise and the potion is yours.

                    BRENDA
          I promise.

(A dinging sound is hear. BRENDA looks around for it as
SNORZ hands her the potion)

                    SNORZ
          Very good. Thank you, my dear.

(SNORZ exits)

                    BRENDA
          What was that strange dinging
          noise?

(HILDA enters with her sweet and sour meter)

                    HILDA
          I'm afraid you lost .1% on that
          deal.

                    BRENDA
          I did. But I didn't mean anything
          by it.

                    HILDA
          But you promised to steal.

                    BRENDA
          I did? (Sighs and frowns) Oh,
          right. I did. Darn you tricky
          wizards. (Stomps her foot angrily.
          Another DING)

                    HILDA
          Ouch, lost .05% on that one.

                    BRENDA
          I'm sorry.

                                          (CONTINUED)

                         HILDA
              Just be careful.
                    (Starts to go)

                         BRENDA
              Wait. How do I get to the Prince's
              castle?

                         HILDA
              You can fly or teleport.

                         BRENDA
              Actually, I'd prefer to walk.

                         HILDA
              Walk?

                         BRENDA
              Well, broom power is creating all
              kinds of pollution in the skies!

                         HILDA
              We wouldn't have the colorful
              sunsets without pollution, my dear.

                         BRENDA
              And teleporting could scare
              someone. I wouldn't want to appear
              in people's gardens and scare them.

                         HILDA
              No, I suppose you wouldn't.

                         BRENDA
              So if you could point the way by
              foot.

                         HILDA
              Fine, just follow the brown brick
              road.

                         BRENDA
              Follow the brown brick road?

    (A bunch of little GNOMES do a can-can as the enter singing)

                         GNOMES
              "Follow the brown brick road.
              Follow the brown brick road.
              Follow, follow, follow, follow,
              follow the brown brick road."

                              HILDA
                    Oh, quiet you crazy Gnomes. Get out
                    of here.

(HILDA throws one of her shoes at them and they scramble off
stage)

                              BRENDA
                    But they were so cute.

GNOMES (off) Thanks!

                              HILDA
                    Watch out for them. They're pests.

(GNOMES rush in)

                              GNOMES
                    We know you are but what are we.

                              HILDA
                    Excuse my while I go turn some
                    gnomes to stone and stick them in
                    somebody's yard.

                              GNOMES
                    Eeek!

(GNOMES run off as HILDA chases them)

                              BRENDA
                    Poor little guys. They don't look
                    like pests at all. Okay, now she
                    told me the way. So I just need
                    to...

(GNOMES rush in)

                              GNOMES
                    "Follow the brown brick road.
                    Follow the brown brick road.
                    Follow, follow, follow, follow,
                    follow the brown brick road."

(HILDA rushes in and GNOMES run off with her exiting behind.
BRENDA starts skipping along)

                              BRENDA
                    Follow the brown brick road. Follow
                    the brown brick road.

                         GNOMES (OFF)
          "Follow, follow, follow, follow,
          follow the brown brick road."

                         HILDA (OFF)
          Stop that!

(BRENDA skips along humming and then a WOLF appears. WOLF is
dabbing his mouth with a small red cloak)

                         BRENDA
          Oh, hello, there.

(WOLF hides red cloak behind his back)

                         WOLF
          Oh!

                         BRENDA
          Sorry, I didn't mean to scare you.

                         WOLF
          Little girls do that to me.

                         BRENDA
          Little girls scare you?

                         WOLF
          All the time.

                         BRENDA
          Why is that?

                         WOLF
          It's all that screaming. Little
          girls scream too much.

                         BRENDA
          I won't.

                         WOLF
          You sure? I am scary. (Makes scary
          arm motion) Grrr.

                         BRENDA
          That wasn't too scary.

                         WOLF
          The last little girl thought so.
          Scared her so bad she dropped this.

(Holds out red cloak)

                    BRENDA
          Poor thing. I bet she will get cold
          without it.

                    WOLF
          I didn't think of that. But she ran
          so fast I doubt we'll catch her.

                    BRENDA
          Maybe this is the time to try a
          little magic.

                    WOLF
          Magic? You a fairy?

                    BRENDA
          I'm a witch actually.

                    WOLF
          A witch? But you're not ugly.

                    BRENDA
          Not all witches are ugly. That's a
          common misconception.

                    WOLF
          Miscon-what?

                    BRENDA
          Misconception. It means people
          believe one thing about you but
          it's not true.

                    WOLF
          I know exactly what you mean.
          People misconwhattionize me all the
          time. Man, you accidentally knock
          down some pig's house with a sneeze
          and that start telling stories
          about you. And now there's this
          little girl and her red hood. Who
          knows what they'll say about this
          one.

                    BRENDA
          Wolves and witches have it tough.

                    WOLF
          That they do.

                    BRENDA
          But maybe I can do a little damage
          control. Set down the cloak and
          stand back.

                                        (CONTINUED)

(WOLF puts down red cloak and backs away)

                    WOLF
          What you going to do?

                    BRENDA
          I'm going to do a return to owner
          spell. (BRENDA does a little dance.
          Polka music plays) Holka Polka!

(Lights flash and zap is heard. Blackout)

                    WOLF
          Ah! I'm blind!

                    BRENDA
          Either I am too or something
          happened.

                    WOLF
          Maybe you returned the moon. I
          wonder who the owner was?

                    BRENDA
          Let's try this again. Holka Polka!

(Lights come up and cloak is gone)

                    WOLF
          Hey, the cloak is gone.

                    BRENDA
          And hopefully back with its owner.

(Crying is heard)

                    WOLF
          Oh, no.

                    BRENDA
          What?

                    WOLF
          Another girl and she doesn't sound
          happy.

                    BRENDA
          Better let me talk to her.

(CINDY enters crying. She's a princess and looks it)

                    WOLF
          I didn't make her cry. I swear.

                    BRENDA
          Are you okay?

                    CINDY
          Not really.

                    BRENDA
          Are you hurt?

                    CINDY
          Only on the inside.

                    BRENDA
          Why are you crying?

                    CINDY
          It's the Prince. He's under a
          sleeping spell.

                    BRENDA
          I know. Isn't it terrible?

                    CINDY
          No one knows what to do.

(BRENDA turns detective. A possible first suspect)

                    BRENDA
          So you know the Prince?

                    CINDY
          Not really. We've never met
          although I live in the castle down
          the street from his.

                    BRENDA
          But aren't you a princess? I
          thought all you princes and
          princesses all hung out together.

                    CINDY
          Normally, yes, but I can't though.

                    BRENDA
          Why not?

                    CINDY
          Because... I'm ugly.

(She sobs some more. But CINDY isn't ugly at all so they're
confused)

                    BRENDA
          You're not ugly.

                    CINDY
          Oh, yes I am. You're just being
          nice.

                    BRENDA
          No, really. You're quite beautiful.

                    CINDY
          But look at this nose and this
          hair!

                    BRENDA
          Both are perfect.

                    CINDY
          Perfectly ugly.

                    WOLF
          I know how you feel!

                    CINDY
          Ah! Who is that?

                    WOLF
          Oh, no. Here comes the screaming.

                    CINDY
          It's a wolf!

                    BRENDA
          Please, no. He's a nice wolf,
          really.

                    CINDY
          There's no such thing.

                    WOLF
          Is so!

                    CINDY
          Ah!

                    BRENDA
          Please, please. Both of you, calm
          down.

                    CINDY
          But he's...

                              BRENDA
          Highly misunderstood.

                              WOLF
          And she's...

                              BRENDA
          Got self-esteem issues.

                              WOLF
          I have self-a-team issues too.

                              CINDY
          You do?

                              WOLF
          Yes. Everyone is always going
          around saying "what a big nose you
          have" and "what big teeth you
          have." It hurts.

                              CINDY
          Oh, poor thing. I'm sorry.

                              WOLF
          It's okay. I just want to go away
          some place where I won't bother
          anyone.

                              CINDY
          You don't bother me.

                              WOLF
          I don't?

                              CINDY
          No, in fact you remind me of a
          doggy I had once. You know what he
          liked?

                              WOLF
          What?

                              CINDY
          This.

(CINDY scratches him behind the ear and he starts thumping
his leg)

                              WOLF
          Oh, that's nice.

(CINDY stops and smiles)

                                                    (CONTINUED)

> BRENDA
> My name's Brenda.

> CINDY
> Nice to meet you. I'm Cindy.

> WOLF
> And I'm the wolf.

> CINDY
> The wolf? You don't have a name?

> WOLF
> Nope. Just "The Wolf."

> CINDY
> How sad. Let's give you a name. How
> about Fido?

> WOLF
> Uh, no.

> CINDY
> Spot?

> WOLF
> Nope.

> CINDY
> I know. Mr. Fuzzy!

> WOLF
> Okay.

> BRENDA
> You like Mr. Fuzzy?

> WOLF
> No, but I want her to stop with the
> name calling.

> BRENDA
> So Cindy, do you know why someone
> would want to put the Prince to
> sleep?

> CINDY
> He's so handsome and brave. I can't
> see why anyone would want to do
> anything to him.

(CONTINUED)

                         WOLF
          Brave?

(WOLF laughs and they look at him)

                         BRENDA
          Why are you laughing?

                         WOLF
          Well, I think the Prince has some
          bravery issues.

                         CINDY
          He does? I don't believe it.

                         WOLF
          He screams louder than any girl.

                         CINDY
          He does not.

                         WOLF
          He ran into me once. And he has
          this high-pitched scream... it
          could break glass.

(CINDY smacks him with a folded up fan she is carrying)

                         CINDY
          Bad, Mr. Fuzzy. Take it back.

                         WOLF
          Hey!

                         BRENDA
          Please you two. Let's not fight.

                         CINDY
          The Prince is perfect in every way.
          Unlike me!

                         BRENDA
          Cindy? Who told you that you're
          ugly? Because you're really not.

                         CINDY
          My sisters.

(From off stage, a shrill voice is heard)

                         EZI (OFF)
          Cindy!

                         CINDY
            Oh, no. It's them.

                         DEZI (OFF)
            Where is she?

                         WOLF
            Who are they?

                         CINDY
            My sisters.

(EZI and DEZI enter. They are princesses too and wear
exaggerated princess costumes, a sharp contrast to CINDY's
tasteful costume)

                         EZI
            Where have you been?

                         DEZI
            No one told you that you could run
            off like that.

                         CINDY
            I'm sorry.

(They mock her)

                         EZI AND DEZI
            "I'm sorry."

                         EZI
            That's all she ever says.

                         DEZI
            We need a little less sorry and a
            little more obedience.

                         CINDY
            Sorry.

                         WOLF
            Don't be sorry. These two need show
            a little respect.

(WOLF steps between CINDY and EZI and DEZI)

                         EZI
            What is that?

                         DEZI
            Looks like a stray dog.

(CONTINUED)

                         CINDY
          This is Mr. Fuzzy.

                         EZI
          Don't name it.

                         DEZI
          Then you'll want to feed it.

                         WOLF
          You two look tasty.

                         EZI
          What?

                         DEZI
          I never!

(BRENDA steps between them all)

                         BRENDA
          Please, everyone. Let's calm down.
          (Turns to EZI and DEZI) Hello,
          princesses. I'm Brenda.

                         EZI
          Brenda?

                         DEZI
          Never heard of you.

                         BRENDA
          I'm the daughter of Splenda. The
          good witch of the South.

                         EZI
          Splenda?

                         DEZI
          Witch?

                         CINDY
          Oh, Splenda's so beautiful. I wish
          had her hair.

                         EZI
          Ha! Never.

                         DEZI
          Not with the head of straw.

(WOLF growls and CINDY calms him with a scratch on the ear)

                                              (CONTINUED)

                    BRENDA
So you two know the prince?

                    EZI
Know him? Ha.

                    DEZI
I'm practically engaged to him.

                    EZI
You wish.

                    DEZI
Don't you dare make moves on my
man.

                    BRENDA
Terrible thing about the sleeping
spell. Any idea why someone might
do it?

                    EZI
Maybe they were worried their
sister was trying to take their
man.

                    DEZI
But he is my man.

                    EZI
Since when?

                    DEZI
Since he gave me that rose at the
ball.

                    EZI
Gave you a rose? He knocked over a
vase and spilled it all over your
shoes.

                    DEZI
It's the thought that counts.

                    BRENDA
So do either you play with magic?
Sleeping spells?

                    EZI
Watch it, witch.

                              DEZI
          We know where you're going with
          this.

                              CINDY
          Please, Brenda. My sisters would
          never do anything to the Prince.
          They both love him so.

                              EZI
          Hush up, Cindy. No one was talking
          to you.

                              DEZI
          Yeah, zip it or we whip it.

                              BRENDA
          I hope that's a figure of speech.

                              EZI
          We find that a good whipping keeps
          little girls in line.

                              DEZI
          Why? What are you going to do about
          it?

                              EZI
          Yeah, wonder witch. Gonna cast a
          spell on us?

                              DEZI
          Gonna turn us into toads?

                              WOLF
          Too late for that.

(CINDY giggles a little at the WOLF's joke. EZI and DEZI
grab her in anger)

                              EZI
          You think that's funny?

                              DEZI
          I think she needs a little time
          out.

                              EZI
          In the dungeon!

                              DEZI
          In chains!

(EZI and DEZI start to drag CINDY out but BRENDA and WOLF
block their exit)

                    BRENDA
          Let her go.

                    EZI
          Stay out of this.

                    DEZI
          This is a family problem.

                    BRENDA
          But you're hurting her.

                    WOLF
          Let her go or answer to Mr. Fuzzy.

(EZI and DEZI mock them)

                    EZI
          Oh, I'm so scared.

                    DEZI
          Big Bad Wolf and Wimpy Witch have
          got us cornered.

                    CINDY
          Please, Brenda. Please, Mr. Fuzzy.
          I'll be okay.

                    EZI
          That's what you think.

(She pulls CINDY's hair)

                    CINDY
          Ow!

                    DEZI
          Now keep quiet.

                    BRENDA
          That's it!

(BRENDA does her dance and music plays. Pulls out her wand)

                    EZI
          Oh, no.

                    DEZI
          She wouldn't.

                                              (CONTINUED)

                         BRENDA
                Holka polka!

(Zap sound and lights go black)

                         CINDY
                What happened?

                         WOLF
                I can't see again.

                         BRENDA
                Why does that always happen?

(Oinking is heard)

                         CINDY
                What's that?

                         WOLF
                Hmmm. Sounds like bacon, I mean
                pigs.

                         BRENDA
                We need some lights. Holka polka!

(Lights come back on and there are two stuffed pigs by
CINDY)

                         CINDY
                Pigs!

                         BRENDA
                Ooops.

                         CINDY
                You turned my sisters into pigs.

                         BRENDA
                I guess I kind of flipped out.
                Sorry. I'll change them back.

                         WOLF
                But I haven't had a bite to eat all
                day.

                         BRENDA
                You will not eat the pig
                princesses.

                         CINDY
                I don't mind.

                         BRENDA
          No, no. I better change them back
          before I get in trouble.

                         CINDY
          Trouble? Aren't witches supposed to
          do things like this?

                         BRENDA
          I'm not. (DING sounds is heard)
          Dang it. Too late.

                         WOLF
          So can I eat them?

                         BRENDA
          No. I'm changing them back anyway.
          Holka polka!
               (Music. Blackout. EZI and DEZI
               are heard screaming)

                         CINDY
          Oh, they're mad. You should have
          left them as pigs.

                         EZI
          What did you do to us?

EZI and DEZI snort like pigs after each thing they say.

                         DEZI
          Yeah, what's going on?
               (Snort)

                         EZI
          I can't see!
               (Snort)

                         DEZI
          Cindy, do something!
               (Snort)

                         BRENDA
          Holka polka! (Lights come on and
          EZI and DEZI have pig noses) Oh,
          no.

                         EZI
          Let's get out of here.
               (Snort)

(CONTINUED)

                         DEZI
          Agreed.
               (Snort)

(EZI and DEZI rush off stage)

                         BRENDA
          I feel terrible now. I better fix
          their noses.

                         CINDY
          Maybe later. I think they'll learn
          something from this.

                         BRENDA
          Oh, it's so hard to be good out
          here. At home it's easy but now I'm
          doing bad things all the time.

                         WOLF
          Welcome to the real world.

                         BRENDA
          I thought this was fairytale land.

                         WOLF
          Bad things always happen in
          fairytale land. Most people blame
          it on the witches, but I blame the
          fairies.

                         CINDY
          The fairies? Why?

                         WOLF
          They're always promising happy
          endings but where's my happy
          ending? All that happily ever after
          seems to be reserved for princesses
          and cute little animals. Especially
          bunnies. Why are rabbits always
          getting happy endings? They're
          rodents, I tell you. Rodents!

                         CINDY
          I never thought about it, but I
          think you're right.

                         WOLF
          I want to see a dragon or a troll
          or even an ogre have a happy
          ending.

                    CINDY
          There was that one ogre.

                    WOLF
          Not any more. Fairy godmother has
          it out for him now. When his wife
          had her babies, she gave him three
          of the cutest triplets you've ever
          seen. And you know what ogres think
          of cute.

                    CINDY

          Poor guy.

                    WOLF
          And triplets. They guy never gets
          any sleep.

                    BRENDA
          Speaking of fairy godmother, what
          is she up to these days, besides
          making ogres miserable?

                    CINDY
          She certainly hasn't been making
          any princesses happy that I know
          of.

                    BRENDA
          Ever since the fairies have talked
          about taking away magic, she's been
          pretty quiet.

                    WOLF
          I heard about that. The witches
          must be pretty upset.

                    BRENDA
          That's why I'm here. The witches
          thought if they could help the
          Prince then we could win back favor
          with the people here.

                    WOLF
          Good luck.

                    CINDY
          I just assumed a witch put the
          Prince to sleep. They didn't?

                    BRENDA
          No, we didn't.

                              (CONTINUED)

                            WOLF
That's a misconfection.

                            CINDY
A what?

                            WOLF
When someone thinks you're one way,
but you're not.

                            CINDY
I know what that's like. Everyone
think princesses are pretty and
happy and fragile. But I'm not.

                            BRENDA
You are pretty, Cindy. Really.

                            CINDY
See. And you probably think I'm
happy too, but I'm not. I'm
downright depressed.

                            WOLF
Need a scratch behind the ear?

(WOLF scratches behind her ear and she thumps her foot)

                            CINDY
Hey, that does help.

                            WOLF
I have to admit, you do look a bit
fragile though.

                            CINDY
See... everyone looks at me and
sees a delicate flower, when in
reality, I'm a deadly fighting
machine ready to strike.

                            WOLF
            (Snickers) Really?

(CINDY does some karate moves and grabs WOLF by the arm and
spins him to the floor in a heap)

                            BRENDA
Are you okay?

                            WOLF
Mommy.

                    CINDY
          I'm so sorry.

                    WOLF
          No, I'm fine.

                    CINDY
          You sure?

                    WOLF
          Sure, sure. I just need a moment to
          get the feeling back in my body.

                    CINDY
          I don't know my own strength.

(They help WOLF up)

                    BRENDA
          You know anyone else around the
          kingdom that might have something
          against the Prince?

                    CINDY
          I can't think of anyone.

                    WOLF
          I've heard all kinds of things
          though. Besides the oink twins,
          there's this servant that has it
          out for the Prince.

                    CINDY
          Really? Who?

                    WOLF
          That one with the big nose.

                    CINDY
          Oh, that one.

                    BRENDA
          Must be quite a nose if you know
          who he's talking about.

                    CINDY
          I feel so bad for him. I know what
          it's like to have a huge nose.

                    BRENDA
          Your nose is tiny.

                    CINDY
          It's huge. I've seen it.

                    BRENDA
          Wait. What kind of mirror do you
          have?

                    CINDY
          Huh?

                    BRENDA
          Is it one with a blue sparkling
          frame?

                    CINDY
          How did you know?

                    BRENDA
          Did your sisters give it to you?

                    CINDY
          Yes, on my birthday a few years
          ago.

                    BRENDA
          That's a trick mirror, Cindy.

                    CINDY
          It is?

                    BRENDA
          It makes people look funny. It's
          gag mirror made by a witch named
          Zorka.

                    CINDY
          Oh, those sisters.

                    WOLF
          Want me to eat them?

                    CINDY
          Maybe.

                    BRENDA
          I thought you didn't eat people.

                    WOLF
          Uh... no. Never.

                    BRENDA
          Let's have a talk with that
          servant. (She waves her wand and
                    (MORE)

                                    (CONTINUED)

                          BRENDA (cont'd)
           does her dance) Holka polka! (Zap
           sound)

                          WOLF
           Hey, the lights didn't go out.

                          BRENDA
           I'm improving.

                          CINDY
           There he is.

(PINOCCHIO enters. He has a huge nose)

                          PINOCCHIO
           What a nice day for a walk.

                          BRENDA
           Actually I made you want to do
           that.

                          PINOCCHIO
           You made me? Like with magic?

                          BRENDA
           Yes. I'm a witch.

                          PINOCCHIO
           I know magic too. (Grabs his nose)
           Ow.

                          CINDY
           What's wrong?

                          PINOCCHIO
           Uh, nothing. (Grabs his nose again)
           Ow.

                          WOLF
           Your nose hurt?

                          PINOCCHIO
           A little.

                          BRENDA
           What can you tell me about the
           Prince?

                          PINOCCHIO
           The Prince? Mr. Sleepy?
                (Laughs)

                    BRENDA
Do you know how might have put him
to sleep?

                    PINOCCHIO
Nope. (Grabs his nose) Ow.

                    CINDY
You sure you're okay?

                    BRENDA
So you don't know how the sleeping
spell happened?

                    PINOCCHIO
Nope. (Grabs his nose) Ow.

                    BRENDA
You know something don't you?

                    PINOCCHIO
I promised not to tell.

                    BRENDA
Tell what? You know who did it?

                    PINOCCHIO
No. (Grabs nose) Ow. Oh, man. I'm
going to get a nosebleed again.

                    BRENDA
Please, tell me what you know. We
can help.

                    PINOCCHIO
Help? You want to help that stuck
up good for nothing brat? Oh, he
makes me so mad. "I'm so handsome.
Everyone love me for it." I'm way
better looking than he is.
        (Grabs nose) Ow.

                    WOLF
Tell you what you know or...

                    PINOCCHIO
Or what?

                    WOLF
Or I'll eat you.

(WOLF jumps on him and bites his arm)

                                        (CONTINUED)

                    PINOCCHIO
          Get off!

                    WOLF
          Hey! You taste like wood.

                    PINOCCHIO
          That's because I'm made out of
          wood.

                    WOLF
          Really bad tasting wood.

                    BRENDA
          You're a wooden boy?

                    PINOCCHIO
          No, I'm ginger bread man. (Grabs
          nose) Ow! (Yells at an invisible
          someone in the sky) That was
          sarcasm.

                    CINDY
          What's with your nose?

                    PINOCCHIO
          Nothing. (Grabs nose) Ow.

                    BRENDA
          Tell us what you know about the
          Prince so we can help him.

                    PINOCCHIO
          Like I want to.

                    BRENDA
          Perhaps you're the one who did it.
          Maybe we'll take you to the
          authorities and let them question
          you.

                    PINOCCHIO
          Fine, fine. Tell you what. The
          person who you really want cast a
          spell on me so I can't tell
          anything about it. But what if I
          bring the Prince to you.

                    CINDY
          Can you do that?

                    PINOCCHIO
Sure. I'll sneak him out and bring
him here. Then you can do your
little witch thing and wake him up.

                    CINDY
Could you, Brenda?

                    BRENDA
I could try. Why can't I just go to
the castle and do it?

                    PINOCCHIO
You think they'll let a witch
anywhere near the castle after all
the bad PR you've had?

                    BRENDA
Good point.

                    PINOCCHIO
I'll be back.

                    BRENDA
Thank you.

                    PINOCCHIO
Happy to help. (Grabs nose) Ow.
(Exits)

                    WOLF
You think he'll really help?

                    BRENDA
I'll just keep bringing him back
here until he does. At least I know
that spell works.

                    CINDY
Can you really wake up the Prince?

                    BRENDA
I don't know but I'll try.

                    WOLF
Here comes somebody?

                    CINDY
Is it the servant with the Prince?

                    WOLF
No, it's a big guy. Sumo wrestler
maybe.

                         CINDY
               It looks like an egg.

(HUMPTY DUMPTY waddles in)

                         BRENDA
               I know you. You're Humpty Dumpty
               aren't you?

                         HUMPTY
               Hi. Aren't you Splenda's daughter?

                         BRENDA
               Yes, I'm Brenda.

                         HUMPTY
               Good to meet you. Us Dumpty's are
               good friends of your family.

                         CINDY
               Didn't you used to work at the
               castle?

                         HUMPTY
               Some of my family did. But not any
               more.

                         CINDY
               Why not?

                         HUMPTY
               That Prince and his royal family
               made sure of that. The Prince
               drives me nuts. I'm glad he's
               asleep. He was always pushing me
               around. I'm going to fall one of
               these days and he'll be sorry.

                         BRENDA
               You're glad he asleep?

                         HUMPTY
               Yes. He's such a bully. Now I don't
               have to listen to him making fun of
               me all the time. He's always making
               up rhymes about me, "Humpty Dumpty
               sat on a wall, Humpty Dumpty can't
               come to the ball."

                         CINDY
               How come you can't come to the
               ball?

                         HUMPTY
          My uncle was a bad egg and upset
          the royalty family.

                         CINDY
          What did he do?

                         HUMPTY
          Well, he used to be the court
          jester. He always cracked them up.

                         WOLF
          Saw that one coming.

                         HUMPTY
          But then he broke a major rule. He
          made a joke about the Prince.

                         CINDY
          Oh, dear. The royal parents don't
          like that.

                         HUMPTY
          They boiled him in oil.

                         BRENDA
          That's horrible.

                         HUMPTY
          He survived but now he can hardly
          move. He just sits there all day
          doing nothing. "Roll me to bedroom
          will you, Humpty," he says. "Roll
          me to the living room, Humpty," he
          says. It's so sad.

                         BRENDA
          And now your family isn't allowed
          in the castle.

                         HUMPTY
          All because that Prince has no
          sense of humor about his hair.

                         CINDY
          Oh, dear. He made fun of his hair?
          He's very proud of his hair.

                         HUMPTY
          I wish I had hair.

                                        (CONTINUED)

                         WOLF
            I have enough for both of us. I'll
            bet I have enough hair on my sofa
            to make you a wig.

                         HUMPTY
            That would be nice.

                         CINDY
            Here comes the servant. He's got
            the prince.

(PINOCCHIO enters pushing in the PRINCE who is asleep.
PRINCE has a hand mirror in his hands folded on his chest.
He also has lipstick mouth prints all over his face from
kisses)

                         HUMPTY
            What's he doing here?

                         BRENDA
            I'm going to try and wake him up.

                         HUMPTY
            Why would you want to do that?

                         BRENDA
            Long story.

                         CINDY
            Please hurry, Brenda. He's been
            asleep for so long.

                         BRENDA
            Here goes. (Get out her wand, does
            her dance, music) Holka Polka!

(There's a fizzle sound rather than a zap. WOLF lifts
PRINCE's hand and lets it drop)

                         WOLF
            Didn't work.

                         HUMPTY
            Oh, well. Let's all go home now.

                         BRENDA
            I have to keep trying.

                         HUMPTY
            No, you don't.

                    PINOCCHIO
        We could lose him somewhere
        instead. Out of sight. Out of mind.

                    HUMPTY
        I like it.

                    CINDY
        I would dare let you do such a
        thing.

                    PINOCCHIO
        Typical princess. They see a
        handsome prince and they swoon.

                    HUMPTY
        (Pretends to be a princess) Oh,
        you're so handsome. Can we go to
        the ball?)

                    PINOCCHIO
        Sure, princess. But take a number.
        You can't expect me to spend the
        entire night with just one
        princess.

                    HUMPTY
        Great imitation.

                    PINOCCHIO
        I mean, how many princesses does
        this guy have on the side?

                    WOLF
        Couldn't Cindy just kiss him awake?

                    CINDY
        Sorry, I'm not that kind of
        princess.

                    PINOCCHIO
        No use. Just about every princess
        in the kingdom has tried already.

(PINOCCHIO pushes PRINCE downstage so they can see that he
has lipstick mouth marks from kisses all over his face)

                    HUMPTY
        Those princesses just couldn't
        resist could they?

                         BRENDA
          Wait. I have a potion. (Pulls out
          potion SNORZ gave her) This should
          work. Stand back everyone.

(Everyone backs away from PRINCE and BRENDA. She throws down
the bottle at the base of the rolling bed the PRINCE is on.
There is a boom sound and the lights go up and down. The
PRINCE yawns and stretches)

                         CINDY
          It worked!

                         HUMPTY
          Darn.

                         PRINCE
          Wow, that's the best night sleep
          I've had in a long time.

                         CINDY
          Are you okay?

                         PRINCE
          Sure. Feel great. And looking good!

(He holds up mirror and looks at himself)

                         WOLF
          You did it, Brenda. Way to go!

                         BRENDA
          But I didn't catch the one who did
          it.

(PRINCE has been checking his hair in the mirror and kisses
it and falls asleep)

                         PINOCCHIO
          He's asleep again.

                         BRENDA
          How did that happen?

                         CINDY
          I don't know. He just fell asleep.

                         BRENDA
          I'm out of potion too.

                         WOLF
          Back to square one.

                                              (CONTINUED)

                    HUMPTY
          Oh, that's so sad. Can we lose him
          now?

                    PINOCCHIO
          We're up on a hill. Just one good
          push! (A rumble is heard) I was
          just kidding. (Grabs his nose) Ow.

                    CINDY
          What is that?

                    BRENDA
          Someone's coming.

(Lights go up and down and then there's darkness and big
poof sound and then happy fairy music. Lights come up and
FGM is there)

                    FGM
          Hello, everyone.

                    CINDY
          Fairy godmother. It's so good to
          see you.

                    FGM
          Oh, hello there. Oh, yes. You're
          shoeless Cindy aren't you?

                    CINDY
          Is that what the fairies call me?

                    FGM
          Afraid so. (Turns to others) So
          what do we think we're doing with
          the Prince?

(PINOCCHIO points at BRENDA)

                    PINOCCHIO
          She made me do it.

                    FGM
          And who are you?

                    BRENDA
          I'm Brenda. Splenda's daughter.

                    FGM
          A witch huh?

CONTINUED: 48.

> BRENDA
> I was sent by the witches to help the Prince.

> FGM
> Steal him is more likely.

> WOLF
> She's trying to help. Really?

> FGM
> Says the wolf. That's makes me feel all better now. What? Will the witch cook him and the wolf eat him? Things are getting very bad here in fairytale land?

> CINDY
> You wouldn't do that, would you Brenda?

> BRENDA
> Of course not. You saw me wake him up. I'm trying to help.

> FGM
> Wake him? You were able to wake him up?

> BRENDA
> Just for a minute.

> FGM
> Did he say anything?

> PINOCCHIO
> Yes, he went on and on about his favorite subject.

> HUMPTY
> Himself.

> FGM
> But he didn't say anything. Anything that might help us figure out who did this to him?

> BRENDA
> I'm afraid not.

> FGM
> How unfortunate.

(EZI and DEZI enter with GUARDS who were playing the GNOMES)

(CONTINUED)

                         EZI
              There she is.
                   (Snort)

                         DEZI
              She's the one.
                   (Snort)

(GUARDS rush over and grab BRENDA)

                         BRENDA
              What's going on?

                         EZI
              You're under arrest.
                   (Snort)

                         DEZI
              To the dungeon!
                   (Snort)

(WOLF jumps to protect BRENDA)

                         WOLF
              Let her go.

                         EZI
              Arrest him too.
                   (Snort)

                         DEZI
              He tried to eat us.
                   (Snort)

                         PINOCCHIO
              And me too.
                   (Touches nose and smiles) See,
                   that's no lie.

                         CINDY
              Please. They were only trying to
              help me. They shouldn't be arrested
              for something I did.

                         EZI
              Good point.
                   (Snort)

                         DEZI
              Arrest her too.
                   (Snort)

(GUARDS surround BRENDA, WOLF, and CINDY and they all
struggle. GUARDS chase them around and the three nearly
manage to escape. But GUARDS manage to get chains and ropes
on them)

                    EZI
          Off with their heads!
               (Snort)

(DEZI points at WOLF)

                    DEZI
          I want a rug made of that one.
               (Snort)

                    WOLF
          I hope I make you itch.

                    BRENDA
          Wait. You can't do this. We didn't
          even have a trial. Fairy Godmother.
          Please.

                    FGM
          She is right, you know. She must
          have a trial.

                    EZI
          A trial?
               (Snort)

                    DEZI
          But who will be the judge?
               (Snort)

                    FGM
          I can do that if there are no
          objections.

                    DEZI
          What about the jury?
               (Snort)

                    EZI
          And the buffet?
               (Snort)

                    HUMPTY
          Buffet?

                    EZI
          I'm hungry.
               (Snort)

                    DEZI
          Don't make a pig of yourself
          please.
                (Snort)

                    FGM
          I think we have enough for a jury.
          Pinocchio, Humpty, Ezi, Dezi and
          the Guards.

                    BRENDA
          But we already know how Ezi and
          Dezi will vote!

                    PINOCCHIO
          Don't worry. I'm on your side.
                (Grabs nose) Ouch.

                    WOLF
          No, he's not. He wants us gone so
          the prince doesn't wake up.

                    PINOCCHIO
          That's not true. I love the Prince.
                (Grabs nose) Ow! Should have
                said like and that wouldn't
                have hurt so much.

                    WOLF
          Well, they're fine with me as long
          as they become a hung jury.

                    BRENDA
          Can't we have others on the jury?
          Ones that might be less
          discriminatory?

                    WOLF
          Yes, less dee-grim-i-tary. I hate
          it when people are dis-crem-i-gory.

                    BRENDA
          So until more jury members are
          found,

(SNORZ enters)

                    SNORZ
          Perhaps I can help.

                    EZI
          A wizard!
                (Snort)

                    DEZI
No wizards or witches.
        (Snort)

                    SNORZ
Why not? Too many witches on the
jury now?

                    HUMPTY
That was a good one.

                    FGM
Will this wizard do?

                    BRENDA
Yes, thank you.

                    FGM
Then let's begin. Someone move the
Prince to a more shady area please.
He's getting a sunburn.

                    PINOCCHIO
With pleasure.

                    HUMPTY
I'll help.

(PINOCCHIO and HUMPTY get PRINCE and roll him to edge of
stage and roll him off happily. Everyone else is getting set
up for the trail, getting chairs, tables a place for judge
so they don't notice)

                    PINOCCHIO
Have a nice trip.

                    HUMPTY
See you next fall.
        (PINOCCHIO and HUMPTY laugh)
        About time I got to say that
        to someone else.

                    FGM
Let the trial of Brenda Witch, The
Wolf, and Princess Cindy begin! How
do you all plea?

EZI and DEZI Guilty! (Snort)

                    BRENDA
Not guilty, your honor.

                              FGM
                    So polite. And what are they
                    accused of?

                              EZI
                    Isn't it obvious?
                         (Snort)

                              DEZI
                    She made us pigs!
                         (Snort)

                              BRENDA
                    I tried to change them back.

                              EZI
                    See, she admits it!
                         (Snort)

                              DEZI
                    To the dungeon!
                         (Snort)

(GUARDS rise up and rush over to BRENDA, WOLF, CINDY)

                              FGM
                    Order! Order! We're not done here.

(GUARDS let them go and are disappointed)

                              BRENDA
                    Thank you, your honor.

                              FGM
                    So one count of misuse of magic.

                              WOLF
                    Sure you want to thank her now?

                              FGM
                    And Mr. Wolf?

                              CINDY
                    Mr. Fuzzy.

                              FGM
                    Mr... Fuzzy. What is he accused of?

                              EZI
                    Trying to eat us.
                         (Snort)

                         FGM
          Same old story. Wolf eating people.
          Will you ever change?

                         WOLF
          Wolves do not eat people.

                         FGM
          Did Mr. Fuzzy try to eat you in
          your human form?

                         DEZI
          Well, sort of.
               (Snort)

                         FGM
          Sort of?

                         EZI
          We were pigs at the time and then
          we had pig noses.
               (Snort)

                         FGM
          Tricky.

                         PINOCCHIO
          He tried to eat me. I've go the
          teeth marks still.

                         WOLF
          You're not human either.

                         PINOCCHIO
          I am so a real boy.
               (Grabs nose) Ow!

                         FGM
          And what about Princess Cindy?

                         EZI
          She's a brat.
               (Snort)

                         DEZI
          And she's the brains behind the
          whole thing.
               (Snort)

                         EZI
          She made the other two do this to
          us.
               (Snort)

                         BRENDA
              No, she didn't. I did it all on my
              own.

                         DEZI
              A confession!
                   (Snort)

                         EZI
              Off with her head!
                   (Snort)

(GUARDS rush to grab BRENDA)

                         FGM
              Order! Order!

(GUARDS let go and are disappointed again)

                         BRENDA
              Please, your honor. I wish to stand
              trial alone. The wolf... I mean,
              Mr. Fuzzy was only trying to
              protect us and Princess Cindy is
              about as innocent as they come.

                         FGM
              Well, let's see what the jury has
              to say.

                         EZI
              I'll vote not guilty for Cindy is
              she promises to hand wash my
              dresses for a month.
                   (Snort)

                         CINDY
              Okay.

                         DEZI
              And you'll clean my comb
              collection?
                   (Snort)

                         CINDY
              Yes.

                         DEZI
              Not guilty.
                   (Snort)

                                              (CONTINUED)

                        PINOCCHIO
          Not guilty.

                        HUMPTY
          Not guilty.

                        SNORZ
          Not guilty.

                        FGM
          You're free to go.

                        CINDY
          Brenda, you don't have to do this
          alone.

                        BRENDA
          It's okay, Cindy. You go.

                        CINDY
          You've been so kind to me. You're
          not what I expected from a witch.

(BRENDA and CINDY hug)

                        EZI
               (Sarcastic) Oh, that's so
               sweet. (Snort)

                        DEZI
          Now go home Cindy!
               (Snort)

                        EZI
          You have a lot of work to do.
               (Snort)

                        CINDY
          Bye, Mr. Fuzzy. If you ever need a
          home, you're always welcome to stay
          at my castle.

(CINDY gives the WOLF on last scratch on the ear and goes)

                        FGM
          Now, for Mr. Fuzzy.

                        EZI
          I guess he didn't actually do
          anything to us.
               (Snort)

                                          (CONTINUED)

                         PINOCCHIO
          He did to me! Now I have to get
          re-sanded now.

                         HUMPTY
          I thought you were a real boy?

                         DEZI
          Let the dog go or we'll never hear
          the end of it from Cindy.
               (Snort)

(Others shrug or nod in agreement)

                         FGM
          Not guilty then. You're free to go
          Mr. Fuzzy.

                         WOLF
          I won't forget how nice you've
          been, Brenda. You witches are all
          right.

                         BRENDA
          Thanks.

(WOLF exits)

                         FGM
          So that leaves you, my dear. Jury?

                         EZI, DEZI, PINOCCHIO
          Guilty!

                         BRENDA
          Don't I get a defense?

                         DEZI
          No.
               (Snort)

                         EZI
          Off with her head!
               (Snort)

(GUARDS grab her)

                         BRENDA
          Wait, all the jury didn't vote.

                         FGM
          Majority rules.

                                          (CONTINUED)

                        BRENDA
          What? You never said that.

                        SNORZ
            Sorry, kid.

(BRENDA gets away from GUARDS and runs to SNORZ)

                        BRENDA
          Can't you help me?

                        SNORZ
          Did you get me a lock of the
          Prince's hair?

                        BRENDA
          No, I didn't have a chance.

                        SNORZ
          Can't keep giving if you don't give
          back.

                        BRENDA
          What do you need it for anyway?

(GUARDS grab her again and SNORZ just smiles)

                        SNORZ
            Bye, kid.

                        BRENDA
          That's it. I'm tired of being Miss
          Nice Witch.
                    (Whips out wands) Holka Polka!
                    (Dance and music) Everybody
                    freeze. (Everyone's feet
                    freeze to the floor. Ding
                    sound is heard) And I don't
                    care about my percent of bad
                    anymore. (Ding) This is so
                    unfair.

                        PINOCCHIO
          What did she do to us?

                        HUMPTY
          Can't... move... Not that I mind.
          Any excuse not the carry this body
          around.

                        EZI
          Do something, Fairy Godmother!
                    (Snort)

                        FGM
          I'm sorry, my dear. But I'm afraid
          I'm going to have to turn you to
          fairy dust.
                    (Pulls out her wand but
                    SPLENDA enters with music and
                    lights)

                        SPLENDA
          Wand!
                    (FGM's wand flies out of her
                    hand) Splendid.

                        FGM
          How dare you!

                        BRENDA
          Mother!

                        SPLENDA
          I came as soon as your sweetest
          dropped too far. What's going on
          here?

                        FGM
          She was trying to escape trial.

                        BRENDA
          It wasn't a fair trial at all.

                        SNORZ
          I would have to agree. Wands!
                    (Zaps SPLENDA and BRENDA's
                    wands away) But I'm not sure I
                    care. (Everyone's feet are
                    unfrozen. EZI, DEZI,
                    PINOCCHIO, GUARDS run)

                        SPLENDA
          What's going on?

                        BRENDA
          I think I know. You're in with the
          Fairy Godmother aren't you?

                        FGM
          You only thought he was a wizard.
          He's really...

                        SNORZ
          The Fairy Godfather.

                                        (CONTINUED)

                        BRENDA
            I've heard of him.

                        SPLENDA
            He's pure evil.

                        BRENDA
            So you two are behind the sleeping
            spell, aren't you?

                        FGM
            Guilty.

                        SPLENDA
            So why did you put the Prince to
            sleep?

                        BRENDA
            It was all a way to make the
            witches look bad.

                        FGM
            And it's worked well.

                        SPLENDA
            As soon as everyone knows!

                        SNORZ
            We can't let that happen.

(HUMPTY sneaks around and picks up SPLENDA and BRENDA wands)

                        BRENDA
            What about the Prince's hair? What
            was that for?

                        SNORZ
            To make the spell permanent.

                        BRENDA
            Why could you get the Prince's hair
            yourself?

                        FGM
            Only one pure of heart can cut it
            for it to work.

                        SPLENDA
            And you're far from it.

                        BRENDA
            So you arranged to have me do the
            deed.

                                        (CONTINUED)

                        SNORZ
        It was too easy.

                        BRENDA
        And now you'll take away magic from
        us and keep it all for yourself.

                        FGM
        Smart little girl. Too bad no one
        is going to find that out.

                        SNORZ
        Shall I... put them to sleep?

                        FGM
        Forever!

(SNORZ gets ready to zap them. HUMPTY rolls in the way,
throws wands to SPLENDA and BRENDA and knocks down SNORZ)

                        HUMPTY
        Strike!

                        SPLENDA
        Wand!

(SNORZ's wand flies away)

                        HUMPTY
        Hold it right there, wizard.

                        BRENDA
        Fairy Godmother is getting away!

(SPLENDA waves her wand)

                        SPLENDA
        Trip!

(FGM trips and falls. BRENDA grabs her)

                        FGM
        That wasn't very nice.

                        SPLENDA
        But you made a splendid crash.

                        FGM
        Witch.

                        SPLENDA
        Fairy.

                    HUMPTY
          Ladies, please.

                    BRENDA
          So who are you?

                    HUMPTY
          Humphrey Dumpty, Private Egg.
          Hard-boiled detective.

                    BRENDA
          So you were just pretending to be
          Humpty?

                    HUMPTY
          I can appear soft-boiled when I
          want to. I was pretending to be a
          disgruntled servant to get in with
          Pinocchio who seems the most guilty
          but then he let me to the real
          brains of the operation. The fairy
          godparents. Let's take these two to
          the dungeon.

                    BRENDA
          Wait. We need their help to wake
          the prince.

                    SPLENDA
          I'll get him.

(SPLENDA waves her wand and PRINCE comes rolling in. He's
covered with branches and leaves from being pushed down the
hill and into the forest)

                    HUMPTY
          Looks like he had a rough ride.

(CINDY and WOLF return)

                    CINDY
          Is everything okay? My sisters came
          home squealing and screaming and
          locked themselves in their towers.

                    WOLF
          And Pinocchio planted himself in
          the forest and is pretending to be
          a tree. I had to see what was up.

                    BRENDA
          I think we have everything under
          control. We just need to convince
                    (MORE)

                        BRENDA (cont'd)
          Fairy Godmother and Fairy Godfather
          to wake the Prince.

                        CINDY
          Fairy Godfather?

                        WOLF
          You're him? The Fairy Godfather?
          He's bad news. You should have seen
          what he did to the King's horses...
          so unless you want me to get all
          the King's horses over here!

                        SNORZ
          No, no. Not the King's horses.

                        HUMPTY
          They are a tough crowd. I always go
          to pieces around them.

                        CINDY
          And fairy godmother. You should be
          ashamed of yourself. You're
          supposed to be helping people. I
          should have known you were no good
          after the way you treated the
          King's men.

                        FGM
          I don't know what you're talking
          about.

                        CINDY
          Maybe we should get the King's men
          and they can tell all about it.

                        FGM
          Not the King's men. Anybody but
          them.

                        HUMPTY
          So unless you want to have a talk
          with all the King's horses and all
          the King's men, I think you need to
          wake up the Prince again.

                        FGM
          Fine. Go ahead and wake him.

                        SNORZ
          I need my wand.

                                              (CONTINUED)

                         SPLENDA
          We'll be watching you close.

(SPLENDA gives him his wand and stands behind him with her
wand to his back)

                         SNORZ
          Awake!

(PRINCE yawns and sits up and stretches)

                         WOLF
          That was easy.

                         SNORZ
          I just make it look easy.

(SPLENDA snatches away his wand)

                         PRINCE
          What a good nap. I hope I don't
          have bed head.

                         CINDY
          You look great.

                         PRINCE
          Don't I always?
               (Looks around) Why was I
               sleeping out here?

                         FGM
          Please, my Prince. Order these
          witches and rabble arrested.

                         PRINCE
          What for? What did they do?

                         HUMPTY
          Nothing. She's the real culprit.

                         PRINCE
          Humpty?

                         HUMPTY
          Humphrey, actually. Detective. The
          King and Queen hired me to find out
          who put a sleeping spell.

                         PRINCE
          Sleeping spell. So that explains
          why I feel so rested.

                                        (CONTINUED)

                    FGM
          See, he feels good. No harm. No
          foul.

                    PRINCE
          What are you talking about?

                    BRENDA
          She's the one who put the sleeping
          spell on you.

                    PRINCE
          You did? I thought you were
          supposed to do nice things.

                    FGM
          I did it for your own good. I only
          did it to teach a lesson about
          controlling your vanity.

                    HUMPTY
          Likely story.

                    PRINCE
          Vain? I'm not vain.

(PRINCE looks at himself in his mirror and falls asleep)

                    CINDY
          Oh, no!

                    BRENDA
          You mean the spell isn't broken.

                    FGM
          I guess not.

                    SNORZ
          I'm afraid that part is permanent.

                    CINDY
          He can never look in a mirror
          again?

                    SNORZ
          Not without falling asleep.

          (SPLENDA gives him his wand) Awake!

(SPLENDA takes wand back)

                         PRINCE
          I've learned my lesson... please...
          How can I do anything without my
          mirrors? How can I do my hair, how
          can check my teeth for any
          imperfections?

                         FGM
          You can have your servants do it
          for you, as usual.

                         PRINCE
          True, but the thought of never
          seeing myself again! Please,
          reverse the spell. All will be made
          right and you can go free.

                         FGM
          Really?

                         HUMPTY
          Sorry, but I'm taking them in. I'm
          afraid her plan went way deeper.
          She had bigger eggs to fry. The
          sleeping spell was only the Easter
          coloring on a much more rotten egg.

(GUARDS enter and HUMPTY points at FGM and SNORZ)

                         FGM
          Please, Prince. Don't let them do
          this to me.

                         PRINCE
          Can you reverse the sleeping spell?

                         SNORZ
          Nope.

                         PRINCE
          Then take them away.

(GUARDS take FGM and SNORZ away)

                         BRENDA
          I will do my best to find a way to
          reverse that sleeping spell.

                         CINDY
          Meanwhile, have I got the perfect
          mirror for you.

CONTINUED :   67.

                    PRINCE
You think you have a mirror that
will work?

                    BRENDA
Right. The trick mirror your
sisters gave you. It might since
it's enchanted. And if it doesn't
work, you know where those fairy
godparents will be if he falls
asleep again.

                    HUMPTY
Doing dungeon duty.

                    CINDY
Could you perhaps escort me home,
Prince?

                    PRINCE
I would be delighting.

                    CINDY
Delighted?
        (She smiles and giggles)

                    PRINCE
Farewell, good people and thank you
for your assistance.
        (CINDY exits with PRINCE)

                    WOLF
She could do better.

CINDY (off) Come on, Mr. Fuzzy.

                    WOLF
Coming. Bye, all.
        (WOLF exits)

                    BRENDA
And thanks for your help, Detective
Dumpty.

                    HUMPTY
It was a hard shell to crack, but I
managed to scramble up enough
evidence to poach me some crooks.

                    BRENDA
Couldn't resist, could you? Ready
mother?

                          SPLENDA
          Ready. You did a Splendid job,
          dear. You made me proud.

                          BRENDA
          Thanks, mom. Shall we walk home?

                          SPLENDA
          Why not?

(BRENDA and SPLENDA exit. HUMPTY steps up. Lights very
slowly fade during following until there is only a spotlight
on HUMPTY)

                          HUMPTY
          It was dark and stormy night in
          fairyland. A night just perfect for
          witches. With fairy godmother in
          the clink, I began to wonder if we
          were ready for a world turned
          topsy-turvy. Sweet witches and
          friendly wolves. Wise wizards and
          princesses with pig noses. It's a
          world gone mad but somehow things
          are looking sunny-side up and we
          may find some kind of happily ever
          after in Fairy Tale Land.

(Detective type music plays as HUMPTY walks out of the
spotlight. Lights fade to black)

                    END OF PLAY

                    OR IS IT?

OPTIONAL EXTENDED ENDING

> HUMPTY (CONT.)
> I was about to call it a day
> because I had this over easy
> feeling coming over me... when she
> rolled in. She had the figure of a
> fortress and the countenance of a
> cobra. She was the goddaughter; the
> witchiest woman west of Walla
> Walla. I wondered if this was some
> kind of yolk. I had already cracked
> the case of the sleeping prince.
> Fairy godmother was left with egg
> on her face. The sleeping spell was
> only the Easter coloring on a much
> more rotten egg. She had bigger
> eggs to fry. And the corruption
> nearly broke fairytale land apart.
> Thankfully they had me to put it
> back together again.
>
> I could continue walking on
> eggshells around her like everyone
> else or I could put all my eggs in
> one basket and say it straight. I
> knew she was trouble and I told her
> so. I told her she was like one of
> those riddles that scramble your
> brains like, "what came first, the
> chicken or the egg?"
>
> I told her to beat it unless she
> wanted to have a talk with all the
> King's horses and all the King's
> men.
>
> But then her eyes teared up and I
> was speechless because I'd never
> seen this cool egg crack before.
> Hey, I've got feelings. I'm a bit
> soft-boiled around the dames. And
> this dame needed help. And help is
> what I do, because I'm
>
> Humpty Dumpty, Private Egg.
> Hard-boiled detective.

TO BE CONTINUED!

SEE THE FOLLOWING PAGES FOR ADAPTED MONOLOGUES AND SCENES
FOR CLASSROOM, AUDITION, COMPETITION OR WORKSHOP

"GOOD DEEDS AND STUFF" MONOLOGUE FOR FEMALE

HILDA
All right, you witches. We've got
ourselves a PR problem here.

Witches have got a seriously bad
reputation here in Fairy Tale Land
and it's only getting worse since
the Hansel and Gretel incident. I
mean, come on people. Eating
children. That's just low.

The fairies are thinking of getting
rid of all magic.

They can and they will unless we
turn things around and prove we can
handle having it.

They gave it to Fairy Tale Land in
the first place. And now they want
it all back because they think we
can't handle it.

We have a crisis here. I mean,
what's a witch without her magic?

We're nothing, I tell you. Nothing!
We'll be just a bunch of creepy old
hags with bad hair and skin.

We have to do a major PR thing.
Good deeds and stuff.

No?

Then say "poof" to your magic and
learn to use chopsticks because
that's all our wands will be good
for.

We need to do a good deed. Not just
any good deed, but a whopper of a
good one.

We're going to save the Prince...
Aka Sleeping Handsome.

But think of the PR. Witches saving
the Prince who has been put under a
sleeping spell. And we must do it
before some bubble headed princess
manages to beat us to it.

"THE BIG BAD WOLF" MONOLOGUE FOR MALE OR FEMALE

                    WOLF
I know exactly what you mean.
People misconwhattionize me all the
time. Man, you accidentally knock
down some pig's house with a sneeze
and they start telling stories
about you. And now there's this
little girl and her red hood. Who
knows what they'll say about this
one.

I have self-a-team issues too.

Everyone is always going around
saying "what a big nose you have"
and "what big teeth you have." It
hurts.

I just want to go away some place
where I won't bother anyone.

They're always promising happy
endings but where's my happy
ending? All that happily ever after
seems to be reserved for princesses
and cute little animals. Especially
bunnies. Why are rabbits always
getting happy endings? They're
rodents, I tell you. Rodents!

"PERFECTLY UGLY" MONOLOGUE FOR FEMALE

(CINDY enters crying. She's a princess and looks it)

                    CINDY
          Am I okay? Not really. No, I am not
          hurt. Well... Only on the inside.
          Something terribly bad and sad
          happened.

          It's the Prince. He's under a
          sleeping spell. No one knows what
          to do. Me? How can I help? Kiss
          him?! I don't even know him. That's
          not proper at all. I'm not that
          kind of princess.

          I live in the castle down the
          street from his but we've never
          met. I always wanted to meet. I saw
          him from my castle tower but I
          never could bring myself to
          introduce myself.

          Because... I'm ugly.

(She cries some more)
          Oh, yes I am ugly. You're just
          being nice. But look at this nose
          and this hair! I am not perfect...
          In any way. Perfectly ugly maybe.

                    END OF SCENE

"HUMPTY DUMPTY PRIVATE EGG HARD-BOILED DETECTIVE" MONOLOGUE
FOR MALE

                        HUMPTY
It was a dark and stormy night in
fairyland. A night just perfect for
witches. With fairy godmother in
the clink, I began to wonder if we
were ready for a world turned
topsy-turvy. Sweet witches and
friendly wolves. Wise wizards and
princesses with pig noses. It's a
world gone mad but somehow things
are looking sunny-side up and we
may find some kind of happily ever
after in fairytale land.

I was about to call it a day
because I had this over easy
feeling coming over me... when she
rolled in. She had the figure of a
fortress and the countenance of a
cobra. She was the goddaughter; the
witchiest woman west of Walla
Walla. I wondered if this was some
kind of yolk. I had already cracked
the case of the sleeping prince.
Fairy godmother was left with egg
on her face. The sleeping spell was
only the Easter coloring on a much
more rotten egg. She had bigger
eggs to fry. And the corruption
nearly broke fairytale land apart.
Thankfully they had me to put it
back together again.

I could continue walking on
eggshells around her like everyone
else or I could put all my eggs in
one basket and say it straight. I
knew she was trouble and I told her
so. I told her she was like one of
those riddles that scramble your
brains like, "what came first, the
chicken or the egg?"

I told her to beat it unless she
wanted to have a talk with all the
King's horses and all the King's
men.

But then her eyes teared up and I
was speechless because I'd never
                  (MORE)

(CONTINUED)

                        HUMPTY (cont'd)
        seen this cool egg crack before.
        Hey, I've got feelings. I'm a bit
        soft-boiled around the dames. And
        this dame needed help. And help is
        what I do, because I'm

        Humpty Dumpty, Private Egg.
        Hard-boiled detective.

"DEADLY FIGHTING PRINCESS" SHORT SCENE FOR 2 ACTORS

                    CINDY
          I just assumed a witch put the
          Prince to sleep. They didn't?

                    WOLF
          No, they didn't. That's a
          misconfection.

                    CINDY
          A what?

                    WOLF
          When someone thinks you're one way,
          but you're not.

                    CINDY
          I know what that's like. Everyone
          think princesses are pretty and
          happy and fragile. But I'm not.

                    WOLF
          You are pretty, Cindy. Really.

                    CINDY
          See. And you probably think I'm
          happy too, but I'm not. I'm
          downright depressed.

                    WOLF
          Need a scratch behind the ear?

(WOLF scratches behind her ear and she thumps her foot)

                    CINDY
          Hey, that does help.

                    WOLF
          I have to admit, you do look a bit
          fragile though.

                    CINDY
          See... everyone looks at me and
          sees a delicate flower, when in
          reality, I'm a deadly fighting
          machine ready to strike.

                    WOLF
               (Snickers)
          Really?

(CINDY does some karate moves and grabs WOLF by the arm and
spins him to the floor in a heap)

                                        (CONTINUED)

                    BRENDA
          Are you okay?

                    WOLF
          Mommy.

                    CINDY
          I'm so sorry.

                    WOLF
          No, I'm fine.

                    CINDY
          You sure?

                    WOLF
          Sure, sure. I just need a moment to
          get the feeling back in my body.

                    CINDY
          I don't know my own strength.

                    END OF SCENE

"MR. FUZZY" SCENE FOR THREE ACTORS

> CINDY
> Ah! Who is that?

> WOLF
> Oh, no. Here comes the screaming.

> CINDY
> It's a wolf!

> BRENDA
> Please, no. He's a nice wolf,
> really.

> CINDY
> There's no such thing.

> WOLF
> Is so!

> CINDY
> Ah!

> BRENDA
> Please, please. Both of you, calm
> down.

> CINDY
> But he's...

> BRENDA
> Highly misunderstood.

> WOLF
> And she's...

> BRENDA
> Got self-esteem issues.

> WOLF
> I have self-a-team issues too.

> CINDY
> You do?

> WOLF
> Yes. Everyone is always going
> around saying "what a big nose you
> have" and "what big teeth you
> have." It hurts.

(CONTINUED)

                         CINDY
          Oh, poor thing. I'm sorry.

                         WOLF
          It's okay. I just want to go away
          some place where I won't bother
          anyone.

                         CINDY
          You don't bother me.

                         WOLF
          I don't?

                         CINDY
          No, in fact you remind me of a
          doggy I had once. You know what he
          liked?

                         WOLF
          What?

                         CINDY
          This.

(CINDY scratches him behind the ear and he starts thumping
his leg)

                         WOLF
          Oh, that's nice.

(CINDY stops and smiles)

                         BRENDA
          My name's Brenda.

                         CINDY
          Nice to meet you. I'm Cindy.

                         WOLF
          And I'm the wolf.

                         CINDY
          The wolf? You don't have a name?

                         WOLF
          Nope. Just "The Wolf."

                         CINDY
          How sad. Let's give you a name. How
          about Fido?

                    WOLF
Uh, no.

                    CINDY
Spot?

                    WOLF
Nope.

                    CINDY
I know. Mr. Fuzzy!

                    WOLF
Okay.

                    BRENDA
You like Mr. Fuzzy?

                    WOLF
No, but I want her to stop with the
name calling.

                    BRENDA
So Cindy, do you know why someone
would want to put the Prince to
sleep?

                    CINDY
He's so handsome and brave. I can't
see why anyone would want to do
anything to him.

                    WOLF
Brave?

(WOLF laughs and they look at him)

                    BRENDA
Why are you laughing?

                    WOLF
Well, I think the Prince has some
bravery issues.

                    CINDY
He does? I don't believe it.

                    WOLF
He screams louder than any girl.

                    CINDY
He does not.

                         WOLF
          He ran into me once. And he has
          this high-pitched scream... it
          could break glass.

     (CINDY smacks him with a folded up fan she is carrying)

                         CINDY
          Bad, Mr. Fuzzy. Take it back.

                         WOLF
          Hey!

                    END OF SCENE

"OW!" A SCENE FOR 3 ACTORS FEATURING PINOCCHIO

(PINOCCHIO enters. He has a huge nose)

                    PINOCCHIO
What a nice day for a walk.

                    BRENDA
Actually I made you want to do
that.

                    PINOCCHIO
You made me? Like with magic?

                    BRENDA
Yes. I'm a witch.

                    PINOCCHIO
I know magic too. (Grabs his nose)
Ow.

                    WOLF
What's wrong?

                    PINOCCHIO
Uh, nothing.
        (Grabs his nose again) Ow.

                    WOLF
Your nose hurt?

                    PINOCCHIO
A little.

                    BRENDA
What can you tell me about the
Prince?

                    PINOCCHIO
The Prince? Mr. Sleepy?
        (Laughs)

                    BRENDA
Do you know how might have put him
to sleep?

                    PINOCCHIO
Nope. (Grabs his nose) Ow.

                    WOLF
You sure you're okay?

(CONTINUED)

                         BRENDA
          So you don't know how the sleeping
          spell happened?

                         PINOCCHIO
          Nope. (Grabs his nose) Ow.

                         BRENDA
          You know something don't you?

                         PINOCCHIO
          I promised not to tell.

                         BRENDA
          Tell what? You know who did it?

                         PINOCCHIO
          No. (Grabs nose) Ow. Oh, man. I'm
          going to get a nosebleed again.

                         BRENDA
          Please, tell me what you know. We
          can help.

                         PINOCCHIO
          Help? You want to help that stuck
          up good for nothing brat? Oh, he
          makes me so mad. "I'm so handsome.
          Everyone love me for it." I'm way
          better looking than he is.
               (Grabs nose) Ow.

                         WOLF
          Tell you what you know or...

                         PINOCCHIO
          Or what?

                         WOLF
          Or I'll eat you.

          (WOLF jumps on him and bites his arm)

                         PINOCCHIO
          Get off!

                         WOLF
          Hey! You taste like wood.

                         PINOCCHIO
          That's because I'm made out of
          wood.

                                          (CONTINUED)

                    WOLF
Really bad tasting wood.

                    BRENDA
You're a wooden boy?

                    PINOCCHIO
No, I'm ginger bread man. (Grabs
nose) Ow! (Yells at an invisible
someone in the sky) That was
sarcasm.

                    WOLF
What's with your nose?

                    PINOCCHIO
Nothing. (Grabs nose) Ow.

                    BRENDA
Tell us what you know about the
Prince so we can help him.

                    PINOCCHIO
Like I want to.

                    BRENDA
Perhaps you're the one who did it.
Maybe we'll take you to the
authorities and let them question
you.

                    PINOCCHIO
Fine, fine. Tell you what. The
person who you really want cast a
spell on me so I can't tell
anything about it. But what if I
bring the Prince to you?

                    WOLF
Can you do that?

                    PINOCCHIO
Sure. I'll sneak him out and bring
him here. Then you can do your
little witch thing and wake him up.

                    WOLF
Can you, Brenda?

                    BRENDA
I could try. Why can't I just go to
the castle and do it?

                                        (CONTINUED)

                        PINOCCHIO
        You think they'll let a witch
        anywhere near the castle after all
        the bad PR you've had?

                        BRENDA
        Good point.

                        PINOCCHIO
        I'll be back.

                        BRENDA
        Thank you.

                        PINOCCHIO
        Happy to help. (Grabs nose) Ow.
        (Exits)

                        END OF SCENE

"PIG NOSE PRINCESSES" SCENE FOR 5 ACTORS

(From off stage, a shrill voice is heard)

                    EZI (OFF)
          Cindy!

                    CINDY
          Oh, no. It's them.

                    DEZI (OFF)
          Where is she?

                    WOLF
          Who are they?

                    CINDY
          My sisters.

(EZI and DEZI enter. They are princesses too and wear
exaggerated princess costumes, a sharp contrast to CINDY's
tasteful costume)

                    EZI
          Where have you been?

                    DEZI
          No one told you that you could run
          off like that.

                    CINDY
          I'm sorry.

(They mock her)

                    EZI AND DEZI
          "I'm sorry."

                    EZI
          That's all she ever says.

                    DEZI
          We need a little less sorry and a
          little more obedience.

                    CINDY
          Sorry.

                    WOLF
          Don't be sorry. These two need show
          a little respect.

(WOLF steps between CINDY and EZI and DEZI)

(CONTINUED)

                          EZI
          What is that?

                          DEZI
          Looks like a stray dog.

                          CINDY
          This is Mr. Fuzzy.

                          EZI
          Don't name it.

                          DEZI
          Then you'll want to feed it.

                          WOLF
          You two look tasty.

                          EZI
          What?

                          DEZI
          I never!

(BRENDA steps between them all)

                          BRENDA
          Please, everyone. Let's calm down.
          (Turns to EZI and DEZI) Hello,
          princesses. I'm Brenda.

                          EZI
          Brenda?

                          DEZI
          Never heard of you.

                          BRENDA
          I'm the daughter of Splenda. The
          good witch of the South.

                          EZI
          Splenda?

                          DEZI
          Witch?

                          CINDY
          Oh, Splenda's so beautiful. I wish
          had her hair.

(CONTINUED)

                    EZI
          Ha! Never.

                    DEZI
          Not with the head of straw.

(WOLF growls and CINDY calms him with a scratch on the ear)

                    BRENDA
          So you two know the prince?

                    EZI
          Know him? Ha.

                    DEZI
          I'm practically engaged to him.

                    EZI
          You wish.

                    DEZI
          Don't you dare make moves on my
          man.

                    BRENDA
          Terrible thing about the sleeping
          spell. Any idea why someone might
          do it?

                    EZI
          Maybe they were worried their
          sister was trying to take their
          man.

                    DEZI
          But he is my man.

                    EZI
          Since when?

                    DEZI
          Since he gave me that rose at the
          ball.

                    EZI
          Gave you a rose? He knocked over a
          vase and spilled it all over your
          shoes.

                    DEZI
          It's the thought that counts.

                         BRENDA
          So do either you play with magic?
          Sleeping spells?

                         EZI
          Watch it, witch.

                         DEZI
          We know where you're going with
          this.

                         CINDY
          Please, Brenda. My sisters would
          never do anything to the Prince.
          They both love him so.

                         EZI
          Hush up, Cindy. No one was talking
          to you.

                         DEZI
          Yeah, zip it or we whip it.

                         BRENDA
          I hope that's a figure of speech.

                         EZI
          We find that a good whipping keeps
          little girls in line.

                         DEZI
          Why? What are you going to do about
          it?

                         EZI
          Yeah, wonder witch. Gonna cast a
          spell on us?

                         DEZI
          Gonna turn us into toads?

                         WOLF
          Too late for that.

(CINDY giggles a little at the WOLF's joke. EZI and DEZI
grab her in anger)

                         EZI
          You think that's funny?

                         DEZI
          I think she needs a little time
          out.

                                              (CONTINUED)

                        EZI
          In the dungeon!

                        DEZI
          In chains!

(EZI and DEZI start to drag CINDY out but BRENDA and WOLF
block their exit)

                        BRENDA
          Let her go.

                        EZI
          Stay out of this.

                        DEZI
          This is a family problem.

                        BRENDA
          But you're hurting her.

                        WOLF
          Let her go or answer to Mr. Fuzzy.

(EZI and DEZI mock them)

                        EZI
          Oh, I'm so scared.

                        DEZI
          Big Bad Wolf and Wimpy Witch have
          got us cornered.

                        CINDY
          Please, Brenda. Please, Mr. Fuzzy.
          I'll be okay.

                        EZI
          That's what you think.

(She pulls CINDY's hair)

                        CINDY
          Ow!

                        DEZI
          Now keep quiet.

                        BRENDA
          That's it!

(BRENDA does her dance and music plays. Pulls out her wand)

                                            (CONTINUED)

                         EZI
          Oh, no.

                         DEZI
          She wouldn't.

                         BRENDA
          Holka polka!

(Zap sound and lights go black)

                         CINDY
          What happened?

                         WOLF
          I can't see again.

                         BRENDA
          Why does that always happen?

(Oinking is heard)

                         CINDY
          What's that?

                         WOLF
          Hmmm. Sounds like bacon, I mean
          pigs.

                         BRENDA
          We need some lights. Holka polka!

(Lights come back on and there are two stuffed pigs by
CINDY)

                         CINDY
          Pigs!

                         BRENDA
          Ooops.

                         CINDY
          You turned my sisters into pigs.

                         BRENDA
          I guess I kind of flipped out.
          Sorry. I'll change them back.

                         WOLF
          But I haven't had a bite to eat all
          day.

                                              (CONTINUED)

                         BRENDA
          You will not eat the pig
          princesses.

                         CINDY
          I don't mind.

                         BRENDA
          No, no. I better change them back
          before I get in trouble.

                         CINDY
          Trouble? Aren't witches supposed to
          do things like this?

                         BRENDA
          I'm not. (DING sounds is heard)
          Dang it. Too late.

                         WOLF
          So can I eat them?

                         BRENDA
          No. I'm changing them back anyway.
          Holka polka!

(Music. Blackout. EZI and DEZI are heard screaming)

                         CINDY
          Oh, they're mad. You should have
          left them as pigs.

                         EZI
          What did you do to us?

(EZI and DEZI snort like pigs after each thing they say)

                         DEZI
          Yeah, what's going on?
               (Snort)

                         EZI
          I can't see!
               (Snort)

                         DEZI
          Cindy, do something!
               (Snort)

                         BRENDA
          Holka polka! (Lights come on and
          EZI and DEZI have pig noses) Oh,
          no.

(CONTINUED)

                         EZI
          Let's get out of here.
                    (Snort)

                         DEZI
               Agreed.
                    (Snort)

     (EZI and DEZI rush off stage)

                    END OF SCENE

               * * * * * * * * * * *

*NOTE: For permission to perform "Holka Polka" or any of the
adapted scenes in this book, you can contact
doug@freedrama.net

               * * * * * * * * * * *

          HOLKA POLKA!

     A Fairy Tale Mystery

     By

     D. M. Larson

     Copyright (c) 2005, 2014 All Rights
     Reserved*

Printed in Great Britain
by Amazon